# My First
# DICTIONARY
## all in colour

J. D. Bevington

illustrated by Jennifer Parsons

TREASURE PRESS

First published in Great Britain in 1977 by
The Hamlyn Publishing Group Limited under the title
*My First Dictionary all in colour.*

This edition first published in Great Britain in 1989 by
Treasure Press
Michelin House
81 Fulham Road
London SW3 6RB

ISBN 1 85051 413 5

Printed in Czechoslovakia.
51169/4

# Note to Parents

This is not just another dictionary with a picture for every word:

**elephant**

Nor is it a dictionary which attempts to *define* the meanings of words:

**elephant** *a very large pachydermatous quadruped with tusks of ivory and a long muscular proboscis.*

This dictionary is quite different.

Here words are *used,* often in the familiar phrases of everyday conversation. To make this as much fun and as natural as possible, children are first introduced to an ordinary family. You can see them on the facing page.

All sorts of interesting and amusing things happen in this family: they go to places and do things. They go, for example, to a fair and a zoo; to the mountains and on holiday; they play indoors and out-of-doors; laugh and get cross; are greedy or sleepy or sad. And, of course, they talk about what they are doing or thinking or feeling.

So in this book, the words and illustrations present events or incidents in this family's life. Words are introduced in alphabetical order and are used in a natural way, either in the descriptive phrases or in conversation. Many of the words are also printed on the colourful and imaginative pictures.

Try going through this book from A to Z with your child, reading it aloud and sharing the experiences. If you talk about the words and encourage him to, you will do much more than help him to spell and use words correctly—you will instil in him a love of language, which is just as important.

Chris

Mum

Dad

Patricia

Ben

Grandpa

Grandma

Rebecca

Katie

David

Kim

Wanda

7

# **a A**

### acorns
Acorns are the fruit of oak trees. Katie found some on the ground. 'Squirrels like to eat them,' said mum.

### acrobat
David is up a tree. 'He is like an acrobat at a circus,' said dad. 'More like a monkey,' said mum.

### aeroplane
A big aeroplane flies over. Do you know what kind it is?

### airport
'It's going to the airport,' said dad. 'Aeroplanes land and take off there.'

### always
Mum doesn't like the noise. She always hates noisy things.

### angry
'That squirrel is angry,' said Rebecca. 'You can see how cross it is!'

### animals
'Do a lot of animals live in the wood?'

### answered
'Yes, Ben,' answered Chris. 'There's plenty for them to eat in a wood.'

### ants
'There are some ants here,' said Ben. 'Are ants animals?' 'Yes,' said mum. 'Ants are insects and insects are animals.'

### any
'I don't like any insects,' said Katie. 'I hope there aren't any ants on me.'

acorns

8

aeroplane

### anywhere
'I can't find my book,' said dad. Can you see his book anywhere?

### apple
Rebecca is eating an apple. Apples are her favourite fruit. She likes red apples. Do you?

### arms
Mum has baby Patricia in her arms.

### arrow
Chris is making an arrow from a stick.

### asleep
'Sssch!' said mum. 'Baby is asleep. Don't wake her up!'

### autumn
Look at the colours of the leaves on the trees. They change colour in the autumn before they fall.

### axe
'Oh, look! There's a man with an axe!' calls David. 'I hope he's not going to cut down this tree.'

apple

axe

ants

9

# b B

### baby
The baby looks happy, doesn't she? Do you like babies?

### back
'Patricia likes to lie on her back and kick,' says mum. 'But she must go back to bed soon.'

### bad
'Did she have a bad night?' asks Rebecca. 'Yes,' mum answers. 'She's cutting a tooth and that gives her a bad pain.'

### badge
Ben has a badge. Have you any badges?

### baker
The baker is at the door. He has bread and cakes with him. 'A large loaf, please,' says Katie.

### ball
Ben is playing with a ball.

### balloon
David is blowing up a big balloon.

### banana
Katie is eating a banana. Do you like bananas?

### bang
There is a loud bang! The balloon bursts.

ball

badge

baby

baker

banana

bee

balloon

basket

belt

## bark
Listen to Kim bark! 'Bow-wow! Woof! Woof!' He does not like bangs. 'Why is Kim like a tree?' asks Chris. 'I know,' says David. 'They both have barks!'

## basket
Kim runs to his basket and jumps in.

## bath
'You need a bath,' says Katie. 'You are a dirty dog!'

## bear
'He looks like a woolly bear,' says Chris. 'But not like baby's teddy bear,' says Ben.

## bee
Wanda jumps up at the window. She's trying to catch a bee.

## begins
The bee begins to buzz.

## behind
'It's gone behind the curtain,' says Rebecca.

## belt
And now grandma comes in. 'Have you seen my belt?' she asks. 'I've lost the belt off my coat.'

## bingo
Where is grandma going? She's going to play bingo. 'I hope you win a prize,' says Katie.

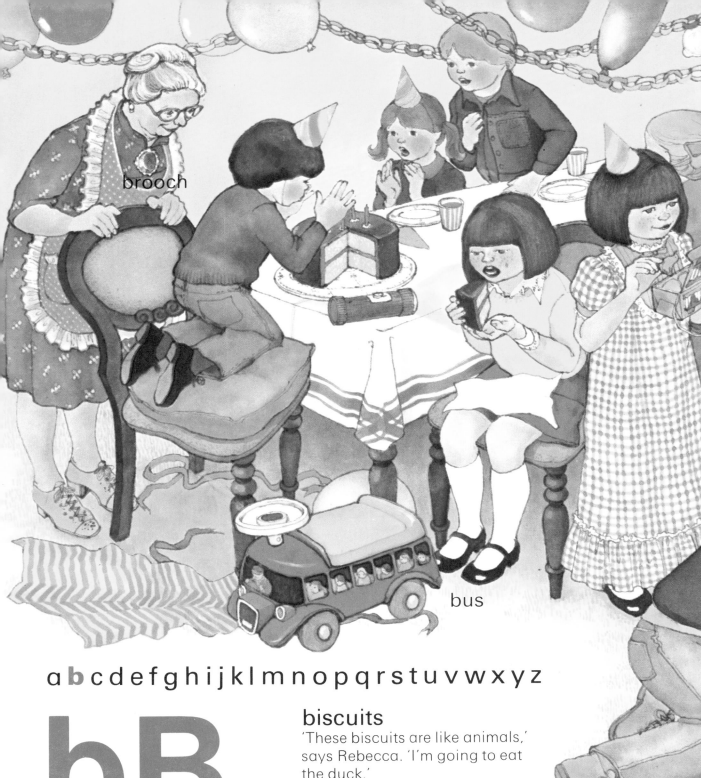

brooch

bus

a **b** c d e f g h i j k l m n o p q r s t u v w x y z

# bB

## birthday
Ben is four today. It is his birthday. Do you like his birthday cake?

## biscuits
'These biscuits are like animals,' says Rebecca. 'I'm going to eat the duck.'

## bite
Katie is hungry. She takes a big bite of cake.

## blow
'Blow, Ben, blow!' Ben blows out the candles – 1 . . . 2 . . . 3 . . . 4.

book

bubbles

box

## boy
Oh dear! A little boy has fallen down and banged his head.

## brave
He does not cry. 'He is a brave boy!' says mum.

## break
She gives him a toy to play with. 'Mind you don't break it,' she says.

## bricks
The big boys have a pile of bricks on the floor.

## bridge
They are making a bridge for the cars.

## bright
Rebecca has given Ben a torch. He shows it to grandma. 'It is bright, Gran, isn't it?' he says.

## brooch
What a pretty brooch grandma has!

## bubbles
A little girl is blowing bubbles. They sail away round the room.

## bus
What does Ben like best? The big red bus.

bricks

bridge

## blue
Ben has a blue jersey. Do you like it?

## boat
Chris has given him a boat with red sails.

## book
Katie has given him a book about the Three Bears.

## box
What is in the big box? It is from David.

boat

# cC

### cage
'We'll go to that cage first,' says grandpa. The cage has big strong bars.

### calf
'I see a baby elephant,' says Katie. 'It's a calf,' says grandpa. 'Baby elephants are called calves.' 'I've got a calf in my leg,' says Katie.

### call
'What do you call the father and mother elephant?' asks Rebecca. 'A bull and a cow,' answers grandpa.

### camel
Rebecca and Katie have a ride on a camel. They sit between its two humps.

### camera
David has his camera. He takes a picture of them.

### cap
'Look at that keeper's cap,' says Chris. 'The wind has blown it away!' All the keepers wear green caps.

### careful
'Those animals bite,' says David. 'You must be very careful, Ben.'

### carry
'Will you carry me, Grandpa?' asks Ben. Grandpa carries Ben on his back.

### catch
An animal gets out of its cage. The keepers soon catch it and put it back.

### cats
'Let's go to see the big cats,' says David. 'Are they bigger than Wanda?' asks Ben. Do you know which animals are called big cats?

### cattle
On the way they pass some cattle with long horns.

### chases
A little one chases after its mother.

### cheetah
The cheetah is in his cage. 'A cheetah is a big cat,' says David. 'It can run very fast.'

### chest
'It's thin, isn't it?' says grandpa, 'but it has long legs and a big chest.'

### children
There are some boys and girls in front of a cage. 'Why are those children laughing?' asks Katie.

### chimpanzee
'They are laughing at the chimpanzee,' says Chris. Can you see what this funny ape is doing?

cheetah

cage

camera

cap

camel

children

chimpanzee

# cC

## chose
'I'm glad we chose to fly in the daytime,' says mum. 'The children can look out of the aeroplane.'

## circles
The aeroplane circles as it rises.

## city
The children look down on the city below them.

## clear
'The air is very clear,' says Chris. 'I can see a long way.'

## climbs
The aeroplane climbs higher and higher.

## close
'Are we close to the sky yet?' asks Ben. 'We're in it,' says dad.

## clouds
'Those clouds look like waves,' says Katie. 'Or like wool,' adds Rebecca.

## coast
Soon they are over the coast, and look down at the sea.

## coffee
Now mum and dad have some coffee.

## cold
The children have cold drinks.

## collar
Dad is hot. He unbuttons the collar of his shirt.

## colour
'The sky is a lovely colour,' says Chris. 'I wish it was always blue.'

## come
'I hope it will be blue,' says mum. 'That's why we come on holiday, and the sun will be hot.'

## cool
'Yes,' says dad, 'but there will be cool winds on the beach.'

## count
'Can you count all the people here, Ben?' asks David.

## crew
'Add the crew as well,' says Chris.

## cross
But Ben is tired and cross. He won't speak.

## cuddles
Mum takes him on her knee and cuddles him in her arms.

16

collar

coffee

a b c **d** e f g h i j k l m n o p q r s t u v w x y z

# dD

## dark
The trees behind the hotel had dark green leaves. 'Are they olive trees?' asked Ben.

## day
'What a lovely day it's been,' said Katie.

## dazzling
The sun was sinking, but was still dazzling.

## deckchair
'This is the life!' said mum, stretching out on her deckchair.

## decorated
The swimming pool was gaily decorated. 'The decorations are pretty,' said Katie.

## deep
Beyond was the deep blue sea.

## delicious
Chris was eating a juicy peach. 'It's delicious,' he said.

## describe
'I'm trying to describe it all,' said David, 'so that we'll remember our holiday.'

## diary
He was writing his diary. He kept it up every day.

## dinner
'Shall we have dinner on the terrace again?' asked Rebecca.

18

diary

## dip
'Have I time for a quick dip in the pool?' asked David.

## disco
'May I go to the disco tonight?' asked Chris.

## display
'Not tonight,' said dad. 'There's to be a display of fireworks this evening.' 'Oh, good!' said the children.

## distance
There was a rumble of thunder in the distance. 'I hope it won't rain,' said Chris.

## donkeys
'Tomorrow,' dad said, 'we are going to see some waterfalls and we are going to ride there on donkeys.' The children were excited.

## dress
'Well, it's time I went to change my dress,' said mum.

## drink
'Let's have a drink first, shall we?' said dad.

## drowsy
'Oh, yes,' said mum. 'I'm feeling a bit drowsy after all the sun and a drink will wake me up.'

## dry
'We're dry too,' cried the children. Dad got them all iced drinks.

19

a b c d **e** f g h i j k l m n o p q r s t u v w x y z

# eE

## eagles
The Eagle's Nest was the name of a rock. People said eagles once nested there.

## early
The bus set off early — before six o'clock.

## east
It took the family up into the hills. 'There's light in the east now,' said David. 'The sun will soon be up.'

## easy
Dad pointed. 'That bit is easy to climb,' he said, 'but it gets harder.'

## eat
'Don't eat your chocolate now, Katie,' said mum. 'You'll be hungry later.'

## echo
David gave a call. They could hear the echo — 'Hello' . . . 'hello' . . . 'hello' . . .

## edge
'Look!' said Rebecca. The stream fell over the edge of some rocks in a waterfall.

## egg
Katie found a broken bird's egg. 'I saw an eagle's egg at the museum,' she said. 'It was as big as your hand, Ben.'

## elbow
Just then Chris slipped. He banged his elbow, but was all right.

## eleven
They had walked a long way. Dad looked at his watch. 'It's past eleven,' he said. 'We'll have a rest.'

## empty
The water flask was empty. 'I'm empty too,' said Katie, rubbing her tummy.

## energy
Mum gave all the children an apple. 'That will give you more energy,' she said. 'And you can eat the chocolate, now.'

## enormous
'Look at that enormous rock,' said Rebecca. 'Can we rest there?'

## excellent
'There's an excellent view of the Eagle's Nest,' said dad, pointing upwards.

## exhausted
'Ben is exhausted,' said mum, but we've all seen the Eagle's Nest!'

## explore
'Can we explore?' asked David. 'Don't go far,' said dad, as Chris and David ran off.

## extra
Mum gave the twins an extra apple. They were still hungry.

## eyes
Mum sat down and shut her eyes. 'Just a little nap,' she said. Ben shut his eyes too. He was very tired.

egg

elbow

# fF

## fair
The fair has come to town, and it's a big one. Do you like fairs?

## family
The whole family go there in the evening.

## far
They park the car. 'It's not far to walk,' says dad.

## fast
David and Chris go on the bumper cars. They like going fast.

## fat
'What does that say?' asks Ben. 'Come and see the Fat Lady,' says mum. 'Does she eat too many sweets?' asks Ben. Mum and dad laugh.

## feathers
'Look at that tall man with feathers on his head,' says Rebecca. 'I think he's a real Red Indian!'

## feel
Now Katie goes on a roundabout. 'I feel sick,' she says when she gets off. And she looks it. 'It's a nasty feeling,' says mum.

## fetches
Dad fetches them all an ice-cream. Katie feels better at once.

feathers

field

## few
'I've only got a few pence left,' says David.

## field
There are booths all round the field.

## fireworks
'Look at all the bright lights!' says Katie. 'They're like fireworks.'

## first
David tries shooting with a rifle. 'You're the first boy to hit it,' says the man.

## fish
Chris tries to catch a fish on a hook, but it keeps falling off.

## five
Dad has a go at the coconut shy. He knocks down two in five throws.

## fix
'Good,' says mum. 'I'll fix one of them up for the birds in the garden.'

# fF

flag

## flag

'What's that boat with the flag, Dad?' asked Chris. 'It's a police patrol boat,' said dad. 'And those yellow flowers are called flags too,' said Katie. 'They are a kind of iris.'

## flaps

From the bank a heron climbed slowly into the air. 'You can count its wing flaps,' said David.

## flash

Suddenly there was a flash of blue. 'A kingfisher,' shouted David.

## flew

'It flew off under those trees.'

## flies

'I don't like all these little flies,' said mum.

## floated

Their boat floated on down the river.

flowers

## flock

They passed a flock of sheep. 'Baa!' said Ben to them, and 'Baa!' they said back to him.

## flood

'There was a flood in those fields last winter,' said dad. 'The water covered them.'

## flowers

Pink and yellow flowers grew along the banks. 'Aren't they lovely?' said mum.

## fluttered

A moorhen fluttered out from the reeds.

## foot

'The water's not very deep, Dad,' called David. He was trailing a foot in the water.

## ford

'I know,' said dad. 'There was a ford here where the horses used to wade across pulling the carts.'

frog

### forward
Mum pointed to a willow tree, as the boat moved forward.

### fresh
'Let's pull in there for tea,' she said. 'The fresh air has made me hungry.'

### fright
They sat on the grassy bank. Rebecca gave a sudden start. 'I had a fright,' she said. 'I thought it was a snake . . .

### frog
. . . but it's only a frog.'

### fruit
Mum gave them all sandwiches and buns. 'And now there's some fruit,' she said.

### full
I'm full,' said dad, rubbing his middle. 'If we eat any more we shall sink the boat!'

### fun
What fun it was!

greenhouse

a b c d e f **g** h i j k l m n o p q r s t u v w x y z

# g G

## game
The children are playing a game in the garden.

## gang
David, Chris, Ben and the girls make a noisy gang.

## gap
Ben hides in a gap in the hedge.

## garage
Nick goes behind the garage door.

## garden
There are lots of places to hide in this garden. Where would you choose?

## gate
'The gate is home,' says David. He waits there while they hide.

## get
'You have to get back here without being touched.'

## give
'I shall give you all one minute,' he says.

garage

grass

### goes
Chris goes off by himself.

### good
Will he find a good place to hide?

### grass
Look at Wanda! She is hiding too. She is hiding in the long grass.

### greenhouse
Can you see Rebecca by the cactus in the greenhouse?

### grins
Grandpa grins at her. 'Mind those prickles,' he says.

### ground
Where is Katie? She is lying on the ground under a bush. She pulls some leaves round her.

### growing
She looks as if she is growing like a plant!

### guard
David looks round. He has to guard the gate, but catch as many of the others as he can. Chris runs from one side and Ben from the other.

### guess
Does he catch anyone? Can you guess who gets home?

27

hole

a b c d e f g **h** i j k l m n o p q r s t u v w x y z

# hH

## half
It is half-past-ten. Mum and dad are going to bed.

## hall
But dad stops in the hall and listens. There is a noise outside. Mum and dad go into the street.

## haze
It is filled with a haze of smoke. Mum and dad bang on the Smith's door.

## head
Mr Smith's head appears at the window.

## heat
But the heat from the flames drives him back. Now the fire-engines arrive.

## heavy
The firemen break down the door with their heavy axes. Two of them go into the shop through the smoke.

## helmet
They are wearing helmets and gasmasks.

## help
'Thank heavens help has arrived in time,' says dad.

helmet

BAKER

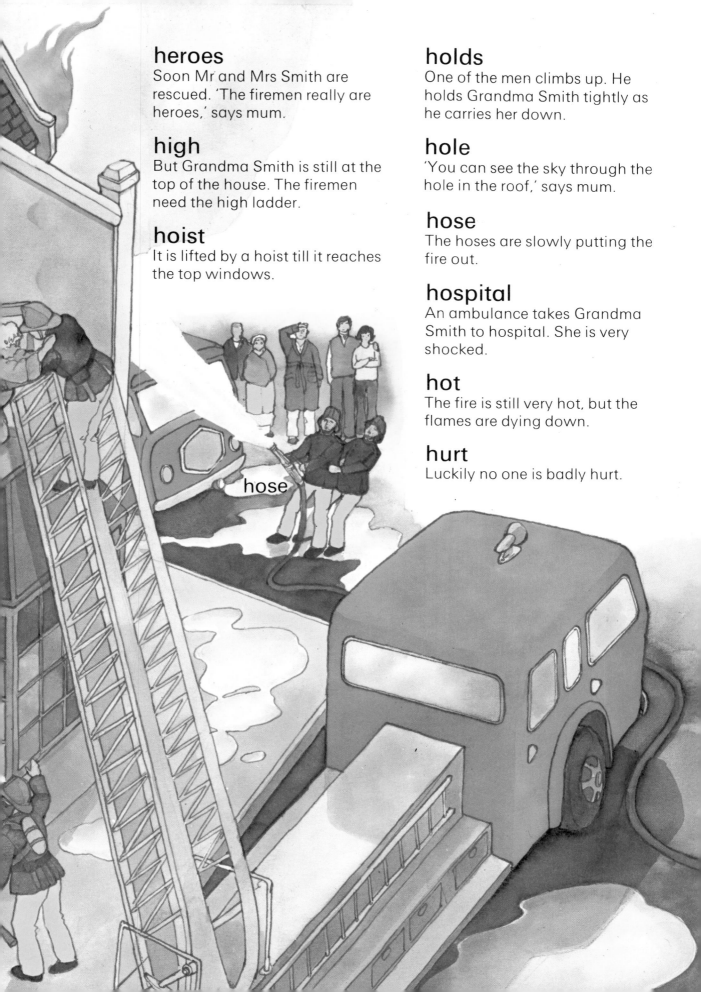

### heroes
Soon Mr and Mrs Smith are rescued. 'The firemen really are heroes,' says mum.

### high
But Grandma Smith is still at the top of the house. The firemen need the high ladder.

### hoist
It is lifted by a hoist till it reaches the top windows.

### holds
One of the men climbs up. He holds Grandma Smith tightly as he carries her down.

### hole
'You can see the sky through the hole in the roof,' says mum.

### hose
The hoses are slowly putting the fire out.

### hospital
An ambulance takes Grandma Smith to hospital. She is very shocked.

### hot
The fire is still very hot, but the flames are dying down.

### hurt
Luckily no one is badly hurt.

hose

a b c d e f g h **i** j k l m n
o p q r s t u v w x y z

## ice
Ben has been stung on the cheek by a wasp. Mum puts some ice on the sting. 'It's all I've got,' she says.

## if
'Come back if you don't feel well.'

## ill
'But stings don't make you feel ill, do they?'

## injection
'And you didn't even mind that injection in your arm last week!'

## insects
'No,' says Ben. 'It doesn't hurt. But wasps are horrid insects, aren't they?'

## inside
'Yes,' mum says. 'I found one inside the marmalade just now.'

## itches
'This sting itches like anything,' says Ben.

## ivy
Just then David calls out from the garden. 'I've found the wasps' nest,' he shouts. 'It's in the ivy.'

ice

jar

jersey

jeans

# j J

### jam
Mum looks for some jam in the kitchen.

### jar
There is a jar on the shelf. She puts it in the garden to trap the wasps.

### jeans
When dad comes home, he puts on some old jeans.

### jersey
. . . and a big jersey.

### jet
He has some poison to kill wasps. He shoots a jet of it into the nest.

### job
'That's a good job done,' says mum.

### joke
Ben's eye goes black. Dad makes a joke about it. 'It looks as if you have been in a fight,' he says.

### jump
Ben laughs. 'The wasp did make me jump, Dad,' he says.

### jungle
'Well,' says dad, 'I must cut back that old ivy. It's like a jungle.'

a b c d e f g h i j **k** l m n o p q r s t u v w x y z

kite

# kK

## keep
'Where do you keep the tea?' asked Katie. 'In that tin,' said mum.

## kettle
She had put the kettle on, and now she called everyone to come to the caravan.

## key
'The key is in the door,' said dad as Ben clambered up the steps.

## kick
'Watch out!' he warned. 'Mind you don't kick the leg of the table.' They all crowded in.

## kind
'It was kind of that man to lend me his fishing rod,' said David.

## kindle
After tea, the children collected sticks for the fire outside. 'It will soon kindle with these dry twigs,' said dad.

## kippers
Soon there was a lovely blaze. 'We'll cook the kippers for supper on it,' said mum.

## kite
'I'm going to fly my kite, now,' said David, running across the field.

## knack
'You'll soon get the knack of it,' called Chris.

## knapsack
Dad got his knapsack from the car.

## kneeling
'What are you kneeling there for?' asked mum.

## knife
'I'm looking for my knife,' said dad, 'to sharpen some sticks.'

## knocked
'We can hang a pan of water on these,' he said to Chris. He knocked the sticks into the ground.

## knots
'Can you make knots?' he asked Chris.

## know
'I know a few,' said Chris. Dad showed him how to make lots more.

knapsack

kettle

knots

knife

kippers

# IL

## label

'What does it say on that label?' asks Rebecca. All the things in the cases are labelled.

## lacewing

'It's a lacewing moth,' says David.'

## lady

'That's a beautiful butterfly,' says Katie. 'Oh, it's called a Painted Lady. Are all butterflies ladies?'

## lapwing

There are some birds in the next case. 'That's a lapwing,' says Chris. 'People call it a peewit too.'

## lay

'Do crocodiles really lay eggs as big as those?' asks Katie.

## lazy

Mum feels lazy. She sits down.

lapwing

## leave
'You can leave me here for a few minutes,' she says. 'I must rest my feet!'

## legs
'Look at that horrid spider,' Katie says. 'Do all spiders have eight legs?'

## length
'Ooh, look at the length of this snake,' says Rebecca. 'It is over three metres.'

## library
Dad points out the library to them.

## life
'People who want to find out about the life of an animal can read books there,' he says.

## like
'I like that ape!' Katie says. 'It's got a kind face.'

## lives
'This animal lives in the Galapagos Islands,' reads David.

## lizard
He was near the huge lizard.

## look
'Look at this,' says dad.

## lose
'Too many have been killed. We don't want to lose any more.'

## lucky
'We are lucky, aren't we,' says David, 'that so many interesting animals still live on the earth.'

library

lizard

# mM

### mackintosh
The children wore coats and dad an old mackintosh to watch the football. 'Your mackintosh will keep you dry,' said mum.

### mad
Ben was mad with excitement. He had never been before.

### made
A kind boy made room for Ben so that he could see.

### make
Soon the crowd began to make a lot of noise.

### man
A man next to David had a loud voice.

### many
'I've never seen so many people,' said Ben. 'How many are there, Dad?' 'About 20,000,' dad answered.

### marched
And now the band marched off the field, and the teams ran on.

### mascot
Ben laughed at a mascot that a boy held up.

### match
It was time for the match to begin. Danny kicked off for the home side.

### men
'Who are the men with flags?' Ben asked. David told him that they put up their flags if the ball was kicked out.

### middle
A man was hurt. He lay down in the middle of the field, near the centre line.

mackintosh

man

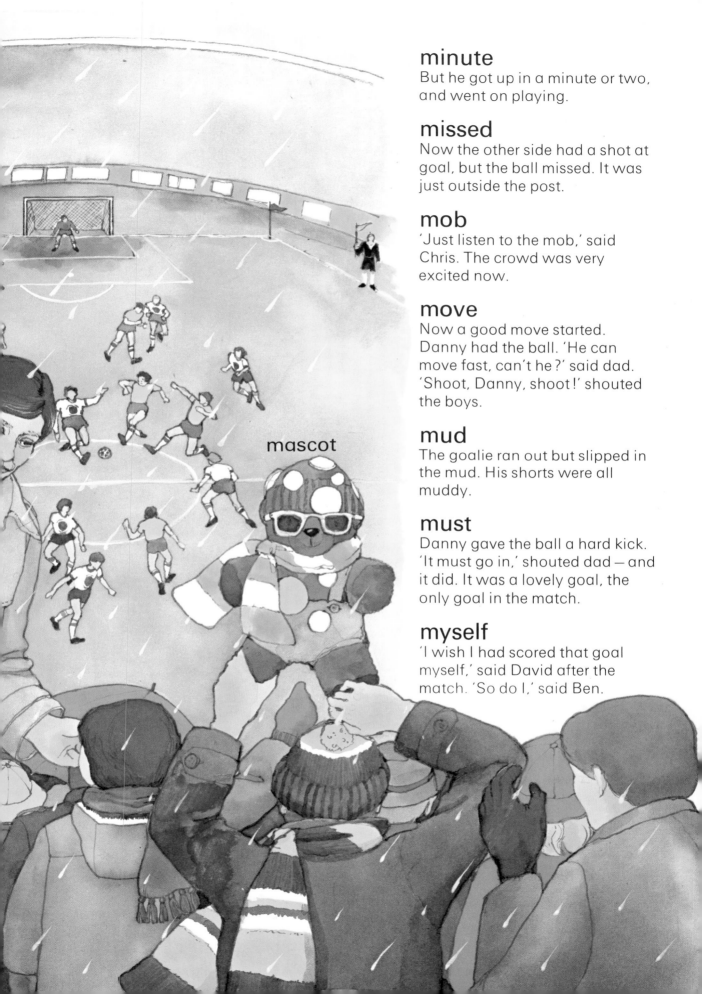

### minute

But he got up in a minute or two, and went on playing.

### missed

Now the other side had a shot at goal, but the ball missed. It was just outside the post.

### mob

'Just listen to the mob,' said Chris. The crowd was very excited now.

### move

Now a good move started. Danny had the ball. 'He can move fast, can't he?' said dad. 'Shoot, Danny, shoot!' shouted the boys.

### mud

The goalie ran out but slipped in the mud. His shorts were all muddy.

### must

Danny gave the ball a hard kick. 'It must go in,' shouted dad — and it did. It was a lovely goal, the only goal in the match.

### myself

'I wish I had scored that goal myself,' said David after the match. 'So do I,' said Ben.

mascot

nurse

# nN

## nail

Nails have sharp points. David was playing in the garden in bare feet when he stood on a rusty nail. The point went into his foot.

## name

Dad took him to hospital. He gave a lady his name and address.

## narrow

The doctor made him lie on a narrow bed while he looked at his foot.

## nasty

'It's a nasty little hole,' he said. 'People shouldn't leave nails lying around, should they?'

## need

'You're going to need an injection,' he said.

## needle

'But don't worry. You'll hardly feel the needle.'

## neglect

'But we mustn't neglect these things. It was a rusty nail.'

## nervous

David felt a little nervous as the doctor got ready.

## nettle

'It won't hurt as much as a nettle sting,' said the doctor. And it didn't.

## next

'I should wear shoes next time you play outside,' said the doctor.

## nodded

David nodded his head. 'I shall,' he said.

## note

The doctor wrote on a note. 'You must have a second injection in about six weeks,' he said.

## nothing

'But you've nothing to worry about now.'

## numb

'Your foot may feel a bit numb for a day or two, and then you'll be as right as rain.'

## nurse

'Just give this note to the nurse as you go out, will you?' 'Thank you very much,' said David.

ote

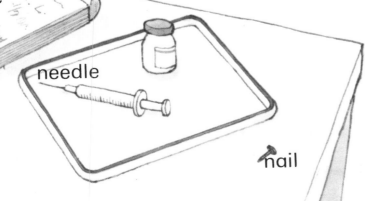

needle

nail

# a b c d e f g h i j k l m n **o** p q r s t u v w x y z

onion

### oak
David is the teacher. 'What sort of wood was used for making ships?' he asks Chris. 'Oak,' says Chris.

### oars
'Now, Rebecca. What do you use for rowing a boat?' 'Oars,' Rebecca answers quickly.

### oasis
'Your turn, Katie. What do you call a place in a desert where you can find trees and water?' 'Is it an oasis?' asks Katie, and David says 'Good.'

### oats
'Now, Ben. What is porridge made from?' Ben says nothing. 'Did you says oats, Ben?' asks David quickly. 'That's a clever boy!'

### oboe
'What is this musical instrument called?' asks David. 'Is it a flute?' 'No. It's an oboe,' answers Chris.

### ocean
'Which is the largest ocean, Rebecca?'·
'The Pacific Ocean,' says Rebecca.

### October
'Katie, what is the tenth month of the year?' Katie counts. 'It's October,' she says. Is that right?

### octopus
'And has an octopus got ten legs, Ben?' asks David. 'No,' says Ben. 'It's got . . . er . . . er . . .' 'Yes, eight legs,' says David quickly. 'Well done, Ben.'

### odd
'It's odd isn't it?' says Katie. 'A spider has eight legs too.' 'And if it loses one, it's got seven,' says Chris, 'and that's an odd number.'

### ogre
'What's an ogre?' 'It's a giant,' Chris answers.

### omnibus
'Rebecca, what is bus short for?' 'Omnibus,' says Rebecca.

### onion
'Katie, what vegetable makes mum cry?' 'An onion, of course,' says Katie, and they all laugh.

### ostrich
'Last question. Why does an ostrich hide its head in the sand?' Nobody knows. Do you know?

### outside
'Let's go outside now,' says David.

### over
'Playing at school is over.'

strich

octopus

odts

oboe

# pP

### page
Katie is at school. She comes to the last page of her book.

### paint
'Now I'm going to paint,' she says. She puts some paint on her brush.

### palace
'What's that?' asks a little boy. 'It's a palace,' Katie says.

### pale
But it's too pale, so she mixes some brighter colours.

### palm
'Now I'm going to paint a palm tree,' she says. 'The queen loves coconuts and they grow on palm trees.' 'My hand has a palm, too,' says a little boy.

### paper
Katie turns the paper over.

### parachute
'What's that in the sky?' asks a boy. 'It's a parachute, of course,' says Katie. 'The king always comes home by parachute.'

page

paper

palace

palm

**parachute**

**pear**

**peacocks**

**picture**

## park
'Look. You can see him landing in the park.'

## patch
'He comes down on that patch of grass near the gate.'

## peacocks
Now a little girl comes up. 'What are those birds?' she asks. 'Oh, they're peacocks,' says Katie. 'Can't you see their tails?'

## pear
She paints a pear tree. It has golden pears.

## peeping
Can you see the little robin peeping through the leaves?

## people
There are some people under the trees.

## pick
'They have come to pick the pears,' says Katie.

## picture
Just then her teacher comes up. 'Have you finished your picture Katie?' she asks.

## pin
'Shall I pin it up on the wall?'

## pink
'This one is nearly finished,' says Katie. 'I just want to give the queen a pink dress.'

pistol

# pP

a b c d e f g h i j k l m n o **p** q r s t u v w x y z

## pirate
Look at the fierce pirate!

## pistol
Can you see the long pistol in his belt?

## plank
He is making the sailors walk the plank.

## play
Who is the pirate? It is David. He is in a school play.

## please
'Keep still, please, Ben,' says mum. But Ben can't keep still.

## plump
'That pirate is a bit plump, isn't he, Mum?' whispers Rebecca.

## pocket
'What's that one got in his pocket?' asks Ben. 'A bottle of rum,' says dad.

## point
Now David draws his cutlass. He feels the point.

## poke
'I hope he doesn't poke that into anyone,' says dad.

## poor
Mum grins. Now the pirates sing a song. 'We take money from the rich and give it to the poor,' they sing. 'Do they really?' asks Katie.

## popular
Everyone likes the song. It is very popular. The pirates have to sing it again.

## port
'What's that red light?' asks Katie. 'It's the port light', says dad. 'Port is the left side of a ship as you look towards the front.' 'I thought port was a drink,' says Rebecca. 'So it is,' says dad. 'It's red too.'

pirate

plank

## powder
'Oh, look, there's Chris,' says Katie. Chris is another pirate. He has a bag of powder for the gun.

## pretending
'He is good at pretending,' says Katie.

## puff
'Now,' says dad, 'the pirates have seen another ship.' There is a puff of smoke as the gun fires. Ben jumps.

## punch
There is a fight as the sailors from the other ship jump on deck. David gives their captain a punch on the nose. But in the end the pirates lose their fight. David is taken away.

## punished
'Will he be punished, Mum?' asks Katie.

## put
'Yes,' says mum. 'He'll be put in prison.'

## puzzled
'Or worse,' says dad. Ben doesn't understand. He looks puzzled.

45

David and Chris are helping Ben
to read. They show him cards
with words and pictures. Ben
looks at the pictures and 'reads'
the words. Can you read the
words without the pictures?

abcdefghijklmnopqrstuvwxyz

# qQ

radio

quarter

rainbow

rhinoceros

queen

ring

queue

rocket

rabbit

racket

# rR

abcdefghijklmnopqrstuvwxyz

# s S

## sack
Chris carried a sack of potatoes into the kitchen. The family helped mum on Sundays.

## safe
David peeled the potatoes with a peeler. 'You're safe with that,' mum said.

## sage
Rebecca got out some sage. 'No, not sage,' said mum. 'It's parsley I want. But sage and parsley are both herbs.'

## salad
Katie did the salad. Mum gave her lettuce and cucumber. 'What are we eating with the salad, Mum?' asked Katie.

## salmon
'I'm making a salmon pie,' said mum. 'It's tinned salmon, of course.'

## salt
David put some salt in the water for the potatoes.

## sample
Katie tasted the pie. 'I'm just trying a sample,' she giggled.

## sandwich
But mum was cross. 'You'll have to have only a sandwich,' she said. 'There's only just enough to go round.'

sack

saucer

scales

salad

## sardine
'A sardine sandwich,' teased Chris, holding up a tin of sardines. He knew Katie hated them.

## sat
Now Wanda came in and sat down close to mum. 'She's smelt the fish,' said mum.

## sauce
'I'm going to make some parsley sauce now. Where did you put the chopped parsley, Rebecca?' asked mum.

## saucer
Rebecca passed her a saucer.

## saw
'Bad cat!' called David, as he saw Wanda reaching for the pie.

## scales
Katie weighed some margarine on the scales.

## school
She had learnt how to use scales at school.

## scrape
Now mum poured out the custard. 'Please scrape out the pan on to Wanda's plate, Chris,' she said.

## scratch
'But use the wooden spoon, or you'll scratch the pan.'

## sends
Lunch is ready. Mum sends all the children to wash their hands.

# sS

### sheets
Washing day! Mum hangs the sheets on the line in the garden.

### shining
'The sun is shining, so they will dry nice and white,' she says.

### shirt
Katie helps her to hang up the boys' shirts.

### shop
'These are the ones we got from that shop when we were on holiday,' says mum.

### shorts
'Will you hang David's shorts up for me?' Katie puts on the pegs.

### shrink
'The man at the shop said they wouldn't shrink,' says mum, 'but it looks as if they have shrunk.'

### silly
'David won't wear them if they look silly,' says Katie.

### sister
'Last one,' says mum. 'Here's your sister's jersey.'

### skipping
'They look as if they are skipping,' says Katie, as the wind blows the clothes.

shorts

sle

skirt

50

sheets

shirt

### skirt
'I'll wash your skirt next week,' says mum.

### sleeve
'Oh, look, that sleeve has come loose.' Katie pegs it up again.

### small
Just then a small white cat walks across the garden.

### smiles
Mum smiles as it rubs against her legs.

### smooth
Rebecca runs up to it. She loves cats. 'How smooth its coat is,' she says, as she strokes it.

### sniffs
Here comes Kim. He sniffs . . . and then he sees the cat. Oh dear! He jumps at the cat . . . but lands in one of the sheets.

### snow
'It was as white as snow,' says Katie.

### soil
'Well now it's all covered in soil from Kim's paws,' says mum.

### some
'Did you see the dog?' asks Rebecca. 'It pulled some washing off the line!'

51

a b c d e f g h i j k l m n o p q r **s** t u v w x y z

# s S

## soon
'It'll soon be better Chris,' says mum.

## sore
But she can see that his arm is sore.

## sorry
'I'm sorry you won't be able to go in today.' 'So am I,' says Chris.

## sound
Now they can hear the sound of children shouting.

## speak
'You can't hear yourself speak!' says Chris.

## spectacles
'Will you look after my spectacles please, Chris?' asks David. He hands Chris his glasses.

## speed
The children change at top speed.

## splashing
Soon they are splashing about in the water.

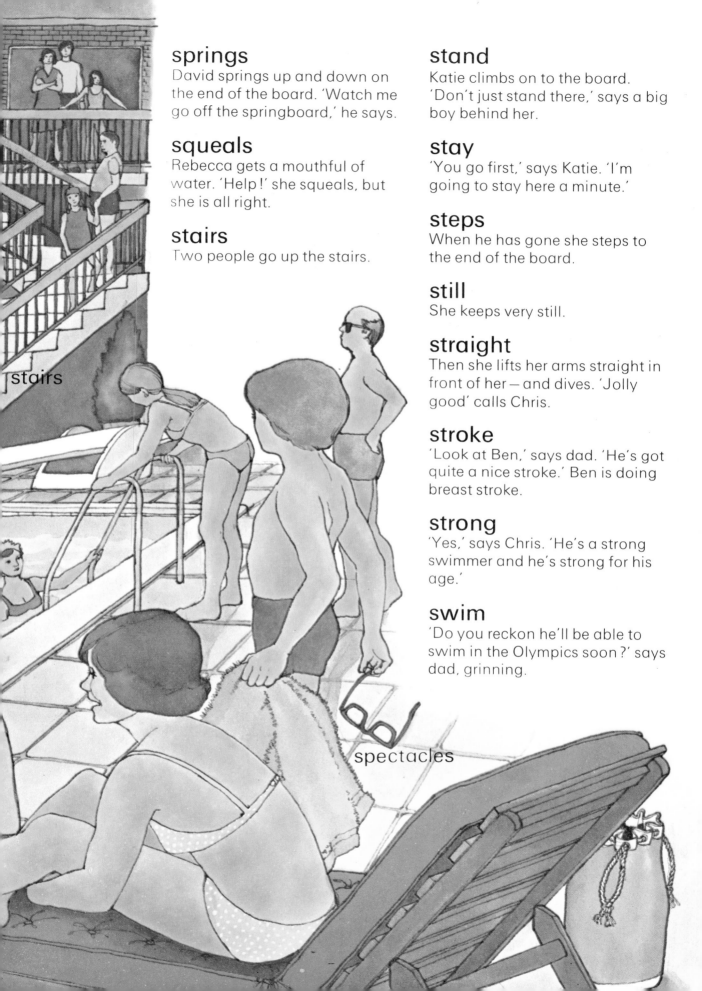

## springs
David springs up and down on the end of the board. 'Watch me go off the springboard,' he says.

## squeals
Rebecca gets a mouthful of water. 'Help!' she squeals, but she is all right.

## stairs
Two people go up the stairs.

stairs

## stand
Katie climbs on to the board. 'Don't just stand there,' says a big boy behind her.

## stay
'You go first,' says Katie. 'I'm going to stay here a minute.'

## steps
When he has gone she steps to the end of the board.

## still
She keeps very still.

## straight
Then she lifts her arms straight in front of her — and dives. 'Jolly good' calls Chris.

## stroke
'Look at Ben,' says dad. 'He's got quite a nice stroke.' Ben is doing breast stroke.

## strong
'Yes,' says Chris. 'He's a strong swimmer and he's strong for his age.'

## swim
'Do you reckon he'll be able to swim in the Olympics soon?' says dad, grinning.

spectacles

trumpet

tulips

a b c d e f g h i j k l m n o p q r s **t** u v w x y z

# tT

## table
Grandma is sitting at the table. She has her handbag with her.

## takes
She takes her purse out of the bag.

## talk
The children come in and sit down quietly. They wait for her to talk.

## tell
'Now, children,' she says, 'I have something to tell you. I won a prize at bingo, and I am going to give you each a little money to spend.'

## ten
She gets out ten coins. 'There are five of you,' she says, 'so you can have two each. Here you are.'

table

tie

cks

## thank
The children thank her very nicely, and the two girls give her a big kiss.

## things
'You must show me the things you buy,' says grandma.

## think
'You must think carefully before you spend the money.'

## thread
Then she gets out a needle and thread and starts to sew.

## three
The three boys got these:

## tie
Chris — a red and blue tie

## tricks
David — a box of tricks

## trumpet
Ben — a trumpet

## tulips
and they bought a bunch of tulips to take back for grandma.

## twins
The twins bought two books each — and

## typewriter
some typewriter ribbon for mum.

# u U

### umbrella
Dad came in from work and put his wet umbrella in the stand.

### uncle
'I've had a letter from uncle Ted — your mother's brother who went to Australia,' he said to the children.

### under
'Don't they call it down under?' said David. 'Yes,' said Chris. 'It's funny to think of Australia under our feet — and it must be funny for Australians to think of us under theirs!'

### understand
'Ben didn't understand — he doesn't know the earth is round.

### undressed
He was undressed and ready for bed.

### uniform
'Uncle Ted is a policeman,' said dad. 'He's sent a photograph of himself in his uniform. Doesn't h look smart?'

### untidy
As uncle Ted's writing was a bit untidy, dad read the letter to the family.

### unusual
The children loved to hear about Sydney, and about the unusual Australian animals — kangaroos wallabies, koalas, duck-billed platypuses, dingoes, wombats and ant-eaters. 'There was a shark off our beach,' dad read, 'and it bit a man's leg.'

### upset
Uncle Ted was very upset about this. But he loved Australia.

### used
'They are getting used to me now,' he wrote, 'and they are all very kind and friendly.'

### utmost
'He sends his love to you all,' da ended, 'and he hopes we'll do ou utmost to save up so we can go out to see him in a few years.' 'That would be lovely,' mum sai

# vV

The children were at a party.

## vanilla

'Do you like ice-cream?' asked the magician. 'You don't like vanilla? Then what about strawberry . . . or chocolate . . . or orange?' The ice-cream changed colour as he talked.

## vanished

Now David gave him his watch. He put a cloth over it and the watch vanished! 'Where is it?' asked David.

## vapour

There was a puff of vapour. There was his watch again!

## vase

And now the magician put a vase of flowers on the table.

## vegetables

'Pretty,' he said, 'but you can't eat them. Let's turn them into vegetables.' He waved his wand. There was a pile of carrots and cabbages on the table.

vase

## ventriloquist

The magician picked up a doll. He talked to it and it answered back. He was a ventriloquist as well as a magician.

## very

'He's very clever, isn't he?' said David. 'I can't see his lips move.'

## voice

'He makes his voice do magic things too,' said Katie. 'I think he's a real magician.'

vegetables

## wades
Chris wades out, pushing his rubber float.

## waist
The sea comes up to his waist. 'Not too far,' calls dad.

## want
'I just want to get to that rock,' shouts Chris.

## warm
The sea is very warm.

## warning
He goes on. He has forgotten the warning about the current.

## watches
Mum watches him.

## water
Dad sees that the water is getting rough.

## waves
There are some big waves.

## way
'Come back!' calls dad. Chris is a long way out now.

## weather
'Oh dear!' says mum. 'The weather is getting bad.'

## where
'Where is the phone box?' asks dad. 'I'm going to get help.'

## while
While he is away, mum calls out, but Chris cannot hear her.

## whistle
Suddenly they hear dad's whistle. He points to the sky. There is a helicopter!

## will
Katie begins to cry. 'Will Chris be all right?' she sobs.

## winch
A man is lowered by a winch just above Chris.

## wind
Another man begins to wind them up.

## window
He pulls them both inside and they wave from the window of the helicopter.

## wonderful
'Well,' says mum, 'isn't that wonderful? Chris is safe.'

## wrapped
Soon Chris is back with the family. He is wrapped in a blanket.

## wrong
There is nothing wrong with him now! 'But I was a bit scared,' he says.

waist

# a b c d e f g h i j k l m n o p q r s t u v w **x** y z

# xX

### x-ray
'I wish I had x-ray eyes,' says David, 'then I could see into the parcels.'

### xylophone
'This one tinkles,' says Chris. 'I think it's a xylophone.'

### Xmas
'Some of my cards say Happy Xmas,' says Rebecca. 'Why do some people call Christmas Xmas?' 'Because they are too lazy to write Christmas,' says dad. 'Or because they forget that it is Christ's birthday,' says mum.

yule-log

zip

# yY

## yacht
'I hope I get a model yacht,' says David.

## yap
'Yap! Yap!' Kim is yapping. He is shut out.

## yawn
Wanda is by the fire. She gives a big yawn.

## year
'Christmas comes only once a year,' says Katie.

## yeast
Mum is making bread. 'I can smell the yeast,' says Rebecca.

## yes
'I like Christmas. Yes! Yes! Yes!' sings Ben.

## yesterday
'Dad stopped work yesterday,' says David. 'It's nice to have him at home.'

## yew
'Look at the lights in the yew trees by the church,' says Katie. 'Aren't they pretty?'

## young
'Baby won't have a stocking,' says Rebecca. 'She's too young.'

## yule-log
Dad comes in. 'This is a yule-log,' he says.

## yule-tide
'Some people still call Christmas, yule-tide.'

## zip
'What have you got for mum?' asks Katie. 'A handbag with a zip,' says dad. 'But don't tell her!'

## zoo
What has dad got for Katie? It's an animal with stripes for her zoo. It begins with Z. What is it?

# zZ